STONER
MUG CAKES

STONER
MUG CAKES

DANE NOON

spruce

An Hachette UK Company
www.hachette.co.uk

First published in Great Britain in 2015 by Spruce,
a division of Octopus Publishing Group Ltd,
Carmelite House, 50 Victoria Embankment,
London EC4Y 0DZ
www.octopusbooks.co.uk
www.octopusbooksusa.com

Distributed in the US by Hachette Book Group,
1290 Avenue of the Americas, 4th and 5th Floors,
New York, NY 10020

Distributed in Canada by Canadian Manda Group,
664 Annette St., Toronto, Ontario, Canada M6S 2C8

ISBN: 978-1-84601-498-7

A CIP catalogue record for this book is available from
the British Library

Printed and bound in China

10 9 8 7 6 5 4 3 2 1

Both metric and imperial measurements have been given
in all recipes. Use one set of measurements only, and not
a mixture of both.

Standard level spoon measurements are used in all recipes
1 tablespoon = 15 ml spoon
1 teaspoon = 5 ml spoon

All microwave information is based on a 650 watt oven.
Follow manufacturer's instructions for an oven with a
different wattage.

Eggs should be medium unless otherwise stated. This book
contains dishes made with lightly cooked eggs. It is prudent
for more vulnerable people such as pregnant and nursing
mothers, invalids, the elderly, babies, and young children to
avoid uncooked or lightly cooked dishes made with eggs.

This book includes dishes made with nuts and nut
derivatives. It is advisable for people with known allergic
reactions to nuts and nut derivatives or those who may be
potentially vulnerable to these allergies, such as pregnant
and nursing mothers, invalids, the elderly, babies, and
children, to avoid dishes made with these. It is prudent
to check the labels of all pre-prepared ingredients for
the possible inclusion of nut derivatives.

CONTENTS

INTRODUCTION

However practiced you are, sometimes the effort of rolling a doobie feels like climbing a mountain. You crave the high but can't muster the energy to peel yourself off the couch, gather your kit, and coordinate your digits to build a passable blunt. You might have the finest gear and a box full of rolling papers, but if your brain isn't sending the right signals to your muscles then that high is going to elude you. If this is a familiar scene, this collection of dope-infused cakes will ensure you've got a constant supply of cheeba in your pantry—edible hits that will get you high and have the bonus of dealing with the munchies at the same time.

HERBAL HISTORY

Although the powers-that-be give stoners a hard time, you're actually following in a long line of "high" achievers. The Chinese Emperor Shen Nung is credited with discovering the medicinal properties of the herb way back in 2700 BC, while the ancient Romans, Greeks, and Egyptians were partial to the odd spliff and cured any number of ills with herb-infused oil. In fact, cannabis has been used throughout history and around the globe to heal and get high.

While Asia and Europe were busy experimenting with cannabis, Americans were a bit late to the party—the marijuana plant didn't make an appearance on US soil until the 17th century. With so much catching up to do, it's no great surprise that weed is America's recreational drug of choice and stateside stoners are serious cannabis connoisseurs.

STRAINS AND STRENGTHS

Every toker has a favorite strain of marijuana and every strain produces a slightly different high. The same rules apply when cooking with cannabis as when smoking it, which means your Nutty Banana Cake might have you crawling up the walls while your buddy's take on Sticky Pear Pudding will see you slide into a cannabis coma. Mug cakes are a movable feast with a virtually limitless variety of highs, depending on your weed of choice and how much of a hit you can handle. You can cook up cakes with any strain of cannabis so you can simply stick to your regular bag or get creative with your shopping list and chop up a new strain of cheeba for your marijuana munchies.

The most widely available and popular strains of weed come from two main varieties—*sativa* and *indica*. There are also hybrids that growers have created by mixing up the varieties to create new strains. For the purposes of time and simplicity, let's stick to the two main strains

SATIVA

This is the plant you'll see on college dorm posters and stoner T-shirts—it has long, slender leaves and plants can top 20 ft (6 m). There are plenty of *sativa* strains to choose from but they will all give a high that literally makes you high—an energetic buzz that should help to get your butt off the couch after a heavy night on the cheeba. These strains tend to be used for daytime smoking.

SATIVA FLAVOR WHEEL

MAUI WAUI
mild/medium hit,
sweet flavor

SHIPWRECK
medium hit,
spicy flavor

KALI MIST
medium hit,
sweet and nutty flavors

WHITE WIDOW
intense hit,
strong earthy flavor

SOUR DIESEL
medium/intense hit,
strong diesel and
earthy flavors

PURPLE HAZE
intense hit,
earthy flavor

LEMON HAZE
intense hit, sweet
and lemon flavors

JACK HERER
intense hit,
woody and
earthy flavors

**SUPER
SILVER HAZE**
intense hit,
sweet and citrus flavors

INDICA

These plants are shorter than their *sativa* cousins. These are the strains to choose if you're looking for total wipeout—your powers of speech and movement will abandon you and your couch will develop a grip that's tighter than octopus tentacles. For that reason, tokers tend to favor *indica* varieties for evening sessions.

INDICA FLAVOR WHEEL

NORTHERN LIGHTS
intense hit, sweet flavor

BLACKBERRY KUSH
medium hit, sweet berry flavor

BLUEBERRY
medium hit, sweet berry flavor

GRANDDADDY PURPLE
intense hit, sweet berry flavor

G13
intense hit, sweet flavor

HOLLANDS HOPE
medium/intense hit, sweet fruit flavor

PURPLE KUSH
intense hit, sweet flavor

BUBBA KUSH
intense hit, earthy flavor

FLAVOR COMBINATIONS

While personal preference or availability is usually the key consideration when it comes to choosing weed, every strain will have a different effect on the overall flavor of your baking, so we've included a recommendation for the type of weed to use at the start of each recipe. These recommendations are split into three categories: sweet, spicy, and earthy.

A flavor wheel (*see* pages 7-8) is the easiest way to come to a decision about which weed to use, but most charts only include a small number of the available strains and hybrids, so here's a more general guide:

SWEET: Kush and small-budded tight *sativas* tend to be sweet and fruity like blueberry, mango, and grapefruit, so use these for a sweet butter.

SPICY: *Indicas* and older strains like the Widows and Jack Herers tend to be more spicy and airy in taste, so use these for a spicy butter.

EARTHY: More informal buds like G13 and hash plant have a more earthy taste and tend to take on flavor as opposed to influencing the overall result, so use these for an earthy butter.

If you prefer the overall taste of your cakes to be less affected by the weed, use one of the more standardized, less fruity and tasty strains—something like Nirvana Northern Light or Blue Mystic.

NO SKILLS REQUIRED

As a seasoned stoner, you've probably sampled a range of cakes, brownies, and cookies that feature the precious herb. But while they may serve the purpose of getting you seriously booted, they're unlikely to win any culinary awards—you probably chow down as quickly as you can, excusing the foul taste in anticipation of the bomb dropping soon after. But with this book, all that will change: now you can savor the flavor of a freshly baked cake, then sit back and wait to get baked yourself.

Of course, when we say "baked" we don't mean anything as complicated as figuring out how to work the oven controls. Dope fiends don't generally list baking as a hobby—reheating a TV dinner is about as close as it gets to home cooking, and that's so long as there's a seriously short list of instructions. But the recipes here are so simple that the last remaining brain cells of the hardcore toker will stay intact and you can enjoy freshly cooked stoner cakes in a matter of minutes using just a handful of ingredients and a couple of everyday kitchen utensils.

Every recipe in the book is mixed in a mug and cooked in the microwave, so you're just one button away from cake heaven and a smooth transition into the ultimate bake break. The ingredient lists are reassuringly short, and you won't need much more than a whisk or a fork to prepare the mix. So, if you're looking for an alternative to rolling and toking, try whisking and chewing your way to your next high and enjoy an intense herbal hit that comes wrapped in a mug cake.

COOKING WITH CANNABIS

The recipes in this book call for either a cannabutter or canna oil to be used as a replacement for standard butter or oil. Before making your weed-infused butter or oil, it is important to "decarb" (decarboxylate) your cannabis. Decarbing is the simple process of heating dried cannabis to the correct temperature in order to create THC (tetrahydrocannabinol), the mind-altering ingredient that gets you high.

HOW TO DECARB YOUR WEED

★ Coarsely grind your weed and then sprinkle it onto a pie dish. Cover well with aluminum foil and crimp the foil along the edge of the dish to seal.

★ Place the covered dish in an oven preheated to 310°F (155°C) and bake for 10–18 minutes. You'll know it is ready when your kitchen smells strongly of weed.

★ Remove from the oven and allow to stand, still covered, until cooled down completely.

HOW TO MAKE CANNABUTTER

1 oz (28 g) decarbed weed (obviously the potency of the butter will depend on the product you use)

2 cups (480 ml) water

2 cups (450 g) unsalted butter

★ Grind your weed to a fine powder using a strong grinder.

★ Pour the water into a heavy-based saucepan and bring to a steady boil over a medium-high heat. Once boiling, add the butter and melt it in the water. Reduce the heat to very low and then whisk in the cannabis powder until thoroughly combined and there are no clumps and nothing is stuck to the bottom of the saucepan. As the butter and water will never mix completely, it is the heat of the water that regulates the heat of the butter. Always make sure there is at least 1½–2 in (4–5 cm) of water between the bottom of the pan and the butter floating on top of it.

★ Cover the mixture with a lid and cook at a VERY gentle simmer for 5–6 hours. During this cooking time you will need to check on the butter mixture every hour to ensure that the simmer is not too strong and that the butter has not reduced too much. If you find the solution reducing faster than expected, add a few extra tablespoons of water. This won't ruin your finished product.

★ Simmer the butter mixture until the fine bubbles stop appearing on the top of the mix (these are an indication of the THC being released from the weed), turn off the heat and allow to stand for 2–4 minutes.

★ Meanwhile, line a large bowl with a square of cheesecloth, making sure the cheesecloth generously overhangs the edge of the bowl. Carefully pour the butter mixture into the cheesecloth-lined bowl and strain off the bits of cannabis. Once you've strained the mixture and the cannabis material is collected in the cheesecloth, carefully squeeze the cheesecloth to extract as much of the butter solution as you can. This is what you want; you can discard the soggy cannabis by-product.

★ Place the bowl of butter solution in your refrigerator and leave to cool for a few hours (or even overnight) until the fats have completely separated from the water.

★ Use heavy-duty plastic wrap to remove the top slab of cannabutter from the bowl and then pat it dry with a paper towel to remove any excess water. Using more plastic wrap, compress the cannabutter into smaller, more manageable portions. Store these little packets in an airtight container in the freezer. If frozen, the cannabutter won't lose any potency before you get around to using it, but it's best used within 2–3 months.

HOW TO MAKE CANNA OIL

2 cups (480 ml) water

3 cups (750 ml) oil (use high-fat oils such as olive oil or coconut oil)

1oz (28 g) decarbed ground bud

★ This process is very similar to making the cannabutter. Start by boiling the water in a heavy-based saucepan over a medium-high heat. Once boiling, add the oil, reduce the heat to very low and slowly add the ground bud into the hot oil and water. Simmer over a very low heat for at least 3–4 hours and a maximum of 24 hours. It's ready when the top of the mixture is thick and glossy.

★ Meanwhile, line a large bowl with a square of cheesecloth, making sure the cheesecloth generously overhangs the edge of the bowl. Carefully pour the oil mixture into the cheesecloth-lined bowl and strain off the bits of cannabis. Once you've strained the mixture and the cannabis material is collected in the cheesecloth, carefully squeeze the cheesecloth to extract as much of the oil as you can.

★ Place the bowl of oil solution in the refrigerator and leave to cool until the oil has completely separated from the water. Once cooled, carefully spoon off the oil and store it in a sealable container in the refrigerator. Use the oil within 6–8 weeks.

EASY DOES IT

Remember that it's harder to control your high when you're getting your kicks from space cakes. Measure the amounts carefully and don't be tempted to throw in the last of the bag—a little goes a long way. When you toke on a spliff, you get a gradual build-up to your high and you can slow down or skip around if you start greening out. With cakes you take the hit in one go, so if the hit's huge you'll be blasted to oblivion when the herb takes hold. For that reason you shouldn't tuck into a whole batch of mug cakes when you're really hungry...unless you want to wipe out and write off the next few days of your life.

GET BAKED CAKES

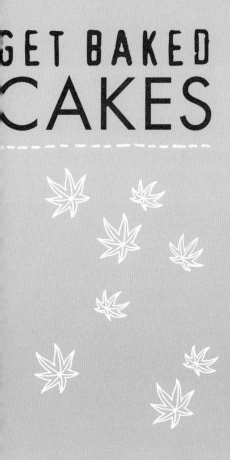

NUTTY BERRY CAKE

RECOMMENDED CANNABUTTER FLAVOR: EARTHY

SERVES	1
PREPARATION TIME	**3 minutes**
COOKING TIME	**2 minutes**

3 tablespoons (40 g) cannabutter, very soft

3 tablespoons superfine sugar

4 tablespoons self-rising flour

1 egg

2 tablespoons pistachio nuts, roughly chopped

10 raspberries, plus extra to decorate

Sifted confectioners' sugar, for dusting

★ Put the cannabutter, sugar, flour, egg, and chopped nuts in a 12 fl oz (350 ml) microwave safe mug and beat together until well mixed. Stir in the raspberries.

★ Microwave on full power for 2 minutes or until the surface feels just firm to touch and a skewer inserted into the center comes out clean. Decorate with extra raspberries and dust lightly with a little sifted confectioners' sugar.

JAMMY SANDWICH

SERVES 1
PREPARATION TIME 3 minutes
COOKING TIME 1½ minutes

3 tablespoons (40 g) cannabutter, very soft

2 tablespoons superfine sugar

1 egg yolk

4 tablespoons self-rising flour

¼ teaspoon vanilla extract

1 tablespoon strawberry preserve

★ Beat together the cannabutter and sugar in a 12 fl oz (350 ml) microwave-safe mug. Add the egg yolk, flour, and vanilla extract and beat together until smooth.

★ Microwave on full power for 1½ minutes or until the surface feels just firm to touch and a skewer inserted into the center comes out clean.

★ Loosen the edges of the cake with a sharp knife and turn out onto a plate. Cut the cake in half horizontally and sandwich the layers together with the preserve.

BLUEBERRY HAZE

RECOMMENDED CANNABUTTER FLAVOR: EARTHY

SERVES 1
PREPARATION TIME **2 minutes**
COOKING TIME **2½ minutes**

1 tablespoon cannabutter

½ cup (50 g) rolled oats

1 tablespoon light brown sugar

2 teaspoons honey

Generous pinch of ground cinnamon

⅓ cup (50 g) blueberries

Greek yogurt, to serve

★ Put the cannabutter in a 7 fl oz (200 ml) microwave-safe mug and microwave on full power for 30 seconds or until melted.

★ Stir in the oats, sugar, honey, and cinnamon and microwave on full power for 1 minute. Mix well, then stir in the blueberries and microwave on full power for 1 minute more or until the blueberry juices start to run. Serve with yogurt.

WEED AND SEED CAKE

RECOMMENDED CANNA OIL FLAVOR: EARTHY

SERVES	1
PREPARATION TIME	2 minutes
COOKING TIME	2 minutes

- 1 egg
- 1 tablespoon canna oil
- 4 tablespoons lemon curd, plus extra to serve
- 1 tablespoon superfine sugar
- 1 teaspoon poppy seeds
- Finely grated zest of ¼ lemon
- 4 tablespoons self-rising flour

★ Beat the egg in a 12 fl oz (350 ml) microwave-safe mug. Beat in the canna oil, lemon curd, sugar, poppy seeds, and lemon zest until well mixed, then stir in the flour.

★ Microwave on full power for 2 minutes or until a skewer inserted into the center comes out clean. Serve with extra lemon curd.

CANDY COMB CAKE

RECOMMENDED CANNABUTTER FLAVOR: EARTHY OR SPICY

SERVES	1
PREPARATION TIME	**3 minutes**
COOKING TIME	**2¾–3 minutes**

1¾ oz (50 g) bittersweet or milk chocolate, broken into chunks

2 tablespoons (25 g) cannabutter

3 tablespoons self-rising flour

1 tablespoon dark brown sugar

1 tablespoon cocoa powder

1 egg

1½ oz (40 g) bag chocolate-coated honeycomb candies

★ Put the chocolate in a 12 fl oz (350 ml) microwave-safe mug and microwave on medium power for 1–1¼ minutes until melted. Add the cannabutter and stir to make a smooth sauce.

★ Add the flour, sugar, cocoa powder, and egg and beat until smooth. Microwave on full power for 45 seconds.

★ Using a rolling pin, lightly crush the honeycomb candies in the bag. Scatter about three-quarters of the crushed honeycomb over the cake and lightly stir in. Microwave on full power for 1 minute more or until just firm to touch. Serve sprinkled with the remaining crushed honeycomb.

CHOC 'N' CHIP CAKE

RECOMMENDED CANNABUTTER FLAVOR: EARTHY

SERVES   1
PREPARATION TIME   **3 minutes**
COOKING TIME   **1¾ minutes**

3 tablespoons (40 g)
  cannabutter, very soft

3 tablespoons superfine
  sugar

1 egg

¼ teaspoon vanilla
  extract

3 tablespoons self-rising
  flour

2 tablespoons bittersweet
  or milk chocolate chips

Sifted cocoa powder,
  for dusting

★ Beat together the cannabutter and sugar
  in a 12 fl oz (350 ml) microwave-safe mug.
  Add the egg, vanilla extract, and flour and
  beat until smooth.

★ Microwave on full power for about 45 seconds
  or until the mixture is just beginning to set.
  Scatter half the chocolate chips over the
  cake and stir once or twice. Scatter over
  the remaining chocolate chips and stir again.
  Microwave on full power for 1 minute more
  or until just firm to touch. Serve dusted with
  a little sifted cocoa powder.

A 'N' R CAKE

RECOMMENDED CANNABUTTER FLAVOR: SWEET

SERVES	1
PREPARATION TIME	3 minutes
COOKING TIME	3 minutes

½ red dessert apple, cored and thinly sliced

2 tablespoons (25 g) cannabutter, cubed

2 tablespoons light brown sugar

2 tablespoons self-rising flour

Finely grated zest of ½ lemon

1 tablespoon golden raisins

1 egg

★ Put the apple in a 7 fl oz (200 ml) microwave-safe mug and sprinkle over the cannabutter and sugar. Microwave on full power for 2 minutes or until the apple juices are bubbling and syrupy.

★ Add the flour, lemon zest, and golden raisins and stir well to combine. Beat in the egg until well mixed.

★ Microwave on full power for 1 minute or until risen and just firm to touch. A skewer inserted into the center should come out clean.

PB&J CAKE

SERVES	1
PREPARATION TIME	**4 minutes**
COOKING TIME	**1½ minutes**

1 tablespoon cannabutter

3 tablespoons crunchy peanut butter

1 tablespoon light brown sugar

2 tablespoons self-rising flour

generous pinch of baking powder

1 egg

2 teaspoons redcurrant jelly

★ Put the cannabutter and peanut butter in a 7 fl oz (200 ml) microwave-safe mug and microwave on full power for 30 seconds. Stir well.

★ Add the sugar, flour, and baking powder and mix until smooth. Beat in the egg.

★ Microwave on full power for 1 minute or until just firm to touch and a skewer inserted into the center comes out clean.

★ Loosen the edges of the cake with a sharp knife and turn out onto a plate. Cut the cake in half horizontally and sandwich the layers together with the jelly.

HOT COFFEE CAKE

RECOMMENDED CANNABUTTER FLAVOR: SPICY

SERVES 1
PREPARATION TIME 5 minutes
COOKING TIME 1½ minutes

½ teaspoon instant coffee granules or powder

½ teaspoon boiling water

3 tablespoons (40 g) cannabutter, very soft

2½ tablespoons superfine sugar

⅛ teaspoon ground cinnamon

Generous pinch of chili powder, plus extra for dusting

1 egg

3 tablespoons self-rising flour

1 tablespoon chopped pecan nuts

heavy cream, to serve (optional)

★ Put the coffee and measurement water in a 12 fl oz (350 ml) microwave-safe mug and mix together. Add the cannabutter, sugar, cinnamon, chilli powder, egg, flour, and nuts and beat together until well mixed.

★ Microwave on full power for 1½ minutes or until the surface feels just firm to touch and a skewer inserted into the center comes out clean. Dust with chili powder and serve with heavy cream, if liked.

SYRUPY PUMPKIN CAKE

SERVES	1
PREPARATION TIME	**4 minutes**
COOKING TIME	**2½ minutes**

- 2 tablespoons (25 g) cannabutter, very soft
- 2 tablespoons superfine sugar
- 1 egg yolk
- 3 tablespoons unsweetened pumpkin purée
- 2½ tablespoons self-rising flour
- ¼ teaspoon vanilla extract
- ½ piece of preserved ginger in syrup, drained and chopped
- 1 tablespoon confectioners' sugar
- 1 teaspoon preserved ginger syrup

★ Put the cannabutter and sugar in a 7 fl oz (200 ml) microwave-safe mug and beat until smooth. Add the egg yolk, pumpkin purée, flour, vanilla extract, and ginger and beat together until well mixed.

★ Microwave on full power for 2½ minutes or until the surface feels just firm to touch and a skewer inserted into the center comes out clean.

★ Beat together the confectioners' sugar and preserved ginger syrup in a small bowl. Drizzle the syrup over the cake and serve.

NUTTY BANANA CAKE

RECOMMENDED CANNABUTTER FLAVOR: SPICY

SERVES	1
PREPARATION TIME	**3 minutes**
COOKING TIME	**2 minutes**

1 small very ripe banana

1 egg

¼ teaspoon ground mixed spice

2 tablespoons (25 g) cannabutter, very soft

3 tablespoons self-rising flour

1 tablespoon chopped walnuts or pecan nuts

2 tablespoons light brown sugar

Maple syrup, to drizzle

★ Mash the banana in a 12 fl oz (350 ml) microwave-safe mug until almost completely puréed. Add the egg, mixed spice, cannabutter, flour, half the nuts, and sugar and beat together until well mixed.

★ Microwave on full power for 2 minutes or until just firm to touch and a skewer inserted into the center comes out clean. Serve scattered with the remaining nuts and drizzled with maple syrup.

GET TOASTED MALLOW CAKE

ERVES	1
PREPARATION TIME	**4 minutes**
COOKING TIME	**1¾ minutes**

- 3 tablespoons (40 g) cannabutter, very soft
- 2 teaspoons light brown sugar
- egg
- tablespoon self-rising flour
- tablespoon cocoa powder
- 5 marshmallows
- oz (25 g) milk chocolate, chopped

★ Put the cannabutter, sugar, egg, flour, and cocoa powder in a 12 fl oz (350 ml) microwave-safe mug and beat together until smooth.

★ Microwave on full power for 45 seconds. Cut four of the marshmallows into quarters. Add the quartered marshmallows and chocolate to the mug and stir gently to mix.

★ Position the remaining marshmallow on top of the mixture and microwave on full power for 1 minute or until the whole marshmallow has partially melted.

TROPICAL SMOOTHIE CAKE

RECOMMENDED CANNABUTTER FLAVOR: SWEET

SERVES 1
PREPARATION TIME 2 minutes
COOKING TIME 2½ minutes

4 tablespoons orange and mango fruit smoothie (or you could use another flavor fruit smoothie)

1 tablespoon cannabutter, very soft

1 tablespoon superfine sugar

1 egg

1 tablespoon self-rising flour

★ Put the fruit smoothie and cannabutter in a 7 fl oz (200 ml) microwave-safe mug and microwave on full power for 30 seconds.

★ Stir in the sugar, egg, and flour and beat together until smooth. Microwave on full power for 2 minutes more.

HIGH CHAI CAKE

RECOMMENDED CANNA OIL FLAVOR: SPICY

SERVES	1
PREPARATION TIME	**3 minutes**
COOKING TIME	**2 minutes**

1 chai teabag

5 tablespoons
boiling water

4 tablespoons mixed
dried fruit

2 dried figs, sliced

¼ teaspoon ground
mixed spice

4 teaspoons canna oil

3 tablespoons self-rising
whole-wheat flour

1 tablespoon turbinado
sugar, plus extra to
sprinkle

★ Put the teabag and measurement water
in a 7 fl oz (200 ml) microwave-safe mug
and stir for 15 seconds. Squeeze the teabag
and discard.

★ Add the dried fruits and mixed spice to
the mug and microwave on full power for
30 seconds. Add the canna oil, flour, and
sugar and stir until mixed.

★ Microwave on full power for 1½ minutes
more or until firm to touch and a skewer
inserted into the center comes out clean.
Sprinkle with a little extra sugar and serve.

FRUIT 'N' NUT CAKE

RECOMMENDED CANNA OIL FLAVOR: SPICY

ERVES	1
REPARATION TIME	**3 minutes**
OOKING TIME	**1½ minutes**

- tablespoons self-rising flour
- tablespoons ground almonds
- teaspoons light brown sugar
- tablespoon canna oil
- tablespoons almond or soy milk
- ew drops of almond extract
- fresh or 5 plump dried apricots, sliced
- teaspoon toasted slivered almonds

★ Mix together the flour, ground almonds, and sugar in a 7 fl oz (200 ml) microwave-safe mug. Stir in the canna oil, almond or soy milk, and almond extract and stir well to mix. Add the apricots to the mug and stir again.

★ Microwave on full power for 1½ minutes or until just firm to touch. Scatter with the slivered almonds and serve.

BEET JUICE MUFFIN

SERVES	1
PREPARATION TIME	3 minutes
COOKING TIME	2 minutes

2 tablespoons fresh beet juice

2 tablespoons (25 g) cannabutter

¼ teaspoon ground cinnamon

2 tablespoons dark brown sugar

2 tablespoons chopped mixed nuts

1 egg yolk

2 tablespoons self-rising flour

To serve
Greek yogurt
Maple syrup

★ Put the beet juice, cannabutter, cinnamon, and sugar in a 7 fl oz (200 ml) microwave-safe mug. Microwave on full power for 30 seconds, then stir.

★ Add three-quarters of the nuts, the egg yolk, and flour and beat together until well mixed. Sprinkle over the remaining nuts and microwave on full power for 1½ minutes or until just firm and a skewer inserted into the center comes out clean. Serve topped with a spoonful of Greek yogurt and drizzled with maple syrup.

GET BAKED CURRANT CAKE

RECOMMENDED CANNABUTTER FLAVOR: SWEET

SERVES	1
PREPARATION TIME	**3 minutes**
COOKING TIME	**2 minutes**

2 tablespoons cornmeal

2 tablespoons (25 g) cannabutter, very soft

2 tablespoons honey

2 tablespoons ground almonds

1 egg

2 tablespoons black currants

1 tablespoon black currant preserve

★ Beat together the cornmeal, cannabutter, honey, and almonds in a 7 fl oz (200 ml) microwave-safe mug. Add the egg and beat together until well mixed.

★ Microwave on full power for 1 minute. Spoon the black currants and black currant preserve on top and stir in lightly so the cornmeal mixture is marbled with the fruit. Microwave on full power for 1 minute more.

HIGH ON DESSERT

DARK CHERRY PUDDING

SERVES	1
PREPARATION TIME	**4 minutes**
COOKING TIME	**2 minutes**

1 oz (25 g) bittersweet chocolate, broken into chunks

2 tablespoons (25 g) cannabutter

1 teaspoon cocoa powder

2 tablespoons light brown sugar

1 egg

6 fresh cherries, pitted and halved

Scoop of vanilla ice cream, to serve

★ Put the chocolate in a 7 fl oz (200 ml) microwave-safe mug. Add the cannabutter and microwave on full power for 45 seconds, stirring once half way through cooking to make a smooth sauce.

★ Stir in the cocoa powder and sugar, followed by the egg, and beat together until well mixed. Stir in the cherries.

★ Microwave on full power for 1¼ minutes or until risen and lightly set. Serve topped with a scoop of ice cream.

STICKY PEAR PUDDING

ERVES	1
REPARATION TIME	3 minutes
OOKING TIME	2¾ minutes

½ small ripe pear

3 tablespoons (25 g) cannabutter, cubed

1 tablespoon light corn syrup

1 tablespoon molasses, plus extra to drizzle (optional)

¼ teaspoon ground ginger

Generous pinch of ground mixed spice

3 tablespoons self-rising flour

1 egg

★ Core the pear. Cut 2 thin wedges of pear and set aside. Dice the remaining pear flesh.

★ Put the diced pear in a 12 fl oz (350 ml) microwave-safe mug. Sprinkle over the cannabutter, then add the syrup, molasses, and spices. Microwave on full power for 1 minute.

★ Add the flour and egg and beat until well mixed. Microwave on full power for 45 seconds. Place the reserved pear wedges on top and microwave for 1 minute more. Serve drizzled with extra molasses, if liked.

FRUITY FUDGE PUDDING

ERVES	1
REPARATION TIME	**3 minutes**
OOKING TIME	**2–2½ minutes**

tablespoons (40 g) cannabutter, very soft

tablespoon light brown sugar

egg

tablespoons self-rising flour

tablespoon golden raisins

oz (25 g) salted fudge, sliced

ight cream, to serve (optional)

★ Put the cannabutter, sugar, egg, flour, and golden raisins in a 12 fl oz (350 ml) microwave-safe mug and beat together until well mixed. Microwave on full power for 1 minute.

★ Add the fudge to the mug and very gently fold into the mixture. Microwave on full power for 1–1½ minutes more or until the surface feels just firm to touch and a skewer inserted into the center comes out clean. Serve with light cream, if liked.

CHOC 'N' CHERRY CLAFOUTIS

RECOMMENDED CANNABUTTER FLAVOR: SWEET

SERVES 1
PREPARATION TIME **4 minutes**
COOKING TIME **3½ minutes**

- 1½ oz (40 g) white chocolate, broken into chunks
- 1 tablespoon (15 g) cannabutter
- 1 teaspoon all-purpose flour
- 3½ fl oz (100 ml) light cream
- 1 egg yolk
- ¼ teaspoon vanilla extract
- 10 canned pitted cherries, drained
- Sifted confectioners' sugar, for dusting

★ Put the chocolate in a 7 fl oz (200 ml) microwave-safe mug. Add the cannabutter and microwave on medium power for 1 minute, stirring once half way through cooking to make a smooth sauce.

★ Add the flour and stir until well mixed, then stir in the cream, egg yolk, and vanilla extract. Finally, stir in half the cherries. Microwave on medium power for 2 minutes or until very lightly set.

★ Scatter the remaining cherries on top of the clafoutis and microwave on medium power for 30 seconds more. Serve dusted with a little sifted confectioners' sugar.

PARADISE PUDDING

SERVES 1
PREPARATION TIME **5 minutes**
COOKING TIME **2 minutes**

2 tablespoons honey

2 tablespoons (25 g) cannabutter, very soft

1 egg

3 tablespoons self-rising flour

½ piece of preserved ginger in syrup, drained and chopped

2 inch- (5 cm-) piece carrot, finely grated

½ fresh or canned pineapple ring, chopped

1 tablespoon preserved ginger syrup, to drizzle

1 tablespoon cream cheese, to serve

★ Put the honey, cannabutter, egg, flour, and ginger in a 12 fl oz (350 ml) microwave-safe mug and beat together until well mixed. Add the carrot and pineapple and mix well.

★ Microwave on full power for 2 minutes or until just firm to touch and a skewer inserted into the center comes out clean. Drizzle with ginger syrup and serve with cream cheese, if liked.

INDEX

GLOSSARY

all-purpose flour : plain flour

beet : beetroot

bittersweet chocolate : plain chocolate

black currant : blackcurrant

confectioners' sugar : icing sugar

cornmeal : polenta

dark brown sugar : dark muscovado sugar

golden raisins : sultanas

heavy cream : double cream

light brown sugar : light muscovado sugar

light corn syrup : golden syrup

light cream : single cream

molasses : treacle

preserve : jam

preserved ginger : stem ginger

rolled oats : porridge oats

self-rising flour : self-raising flour

slivered almonds : flaked almonds

superfine sugar : caster suger

turbinado sugar : demerara sugar

zest : rind